GREAT SMOKY MOUNTAINS NATIONAL PARK

© Published by Aerial Photography Services, Inc.
2511 South Tryon Street
Charlotte, N.C. 28203-4995
Phone (704)333-5143, Fax (704)333-5148
Copyright 1995 by Aerial Photography Services, Inc.
I.S.B.N. 1-880970-16-3

Editors: Beth Dover and Catherine Joseph
Photography by Jim Doane, Bill Tuttle, Fred Eldridge, & Lewis Crisp
Design by Werner J. Bertsch and Jim Doane
Color prints are available from most of the pictures in this book.
Printed in Italy by

THE GREAT SMOKY MOUNTAINS FOUR SEASONS OF SPLENDOR

The most popular National Park in America - 800 square miles of territory - about 60 miles in length, 20 miles in width that straddles the West border of North Carolina and East border of Tennessee.

A magnificent location of Vacation Land for the crowded East of our Nation. Nearly 12 million visitors a year - more than twice the number that visit any other national park in America.

AND YOU MAY WONDER, WHY?

Our geologists tell us that over two hundred million years ago, there was a great upheaval of the Earth's surface in this Appalachian area and the Great Smokies was formed from a shallow sea. For these millions of years, erosion of water and wind did its work. Valleys and slopes, which exist today were formed - and now we have 16 peaks over 6,000 feet and 53 over 5,000 feet in height. The valleys range from a low point of 857 feet at Abrams Creek on the West and ascends in a broken array of valleys and peaks to a height of 6,642 feet at Clingmans Dome, the highest mountain in the park.

All this forms a panorama of beauty. Within its borders you will find deep gorges, gentle slopes, rapid streams, clear pools, jagged rocks, great forests and rich meadows.

Plant life is in profusion. You will find 1,300 kinds of flowering shrubs and plants, 130 different kinds of trees, nearly 30 varieties of orchids and grasses of all kinds. Nourished by a rich soil, a heavy rainfall (about 80 inches), and the sun of our most temperate zone makes the area of this park one of the most luxuriant of the World, the Kashmir, The Shangri-La of America.

This profuse growth of vegetation (being close packed Rhododendron and Mountain Laurel) combines with the oil of the pines to exude an aroma and a vapor that rises and mixes with the feathery fleece of the fog. It clings to the top of the mountain and sinks to the Valley below, and you have the Smokies, and the reason for the name, The Great Smoky Mountains National Park.

It is no wonder that our feathery friends, the fish that like clear waters and the animals of the hills and glens come to this park and join with us, the People, in making this park their haven and refuge.

Let us tell you how the Smokies became one of our national Parks. As you know, most all of our other parks were set aside from government lands and before the private individual could claim any ownership therein.

However, with the Smokies it was different. For years its land was owned by private individuals and lumber companies as it contained one of the finest spreads of lumber in the United States. Spruce, fir and hemlock, oak, walnut and other fine woods grew straight and tall. Then came the devastating forces of man in his search for the dollar. Private enterprise in the form of saw mills was beginning to destroy one of the beautiful wilderness areas of the nation.

Lucky for all of us, one of the reasons we are a great nation and people is that in time of need there has always been an individual who has come to our rescue. In this case a woman, Mrs. Willis P. Davis of Knoxville, Tennessee, realizing the grandeur of the area started a movement to change the entire complex to a National Park. Others followed, and John D. Rockfeller, Jr. (a member of a family that has, and is still giving millions to areas where there is need and where the public welfare may be enhanced), contributed $ 5,000,000.00. This amount was added to funds from State, Federal and Private Sources and the lands of the Smokies was purchased and given to the Federal Government. On September 8, 1940, the Great Smoky Mountains National Park became a reality when it was formally dedicated by President Franklin D. Roosevelt.

Yes, the great lumber camps of the Smokies were stilled and the wealth of this area was channeled to a place of relaxation, a place of beauty, a place of refuge to all who may come.

And this America, our home, the home of over two hundred and seventy million people like us, was taught the lesson.

"There are times when we must call a halt to the destruction of our resources, we must give nature a chance, for in her grand design she has built peaks and great gorges, and peaceful valleys, clear lakes and rapid streams. These just don't belong to us, but to others who may come and must keep this grand design unspoiled".

The Peace in these Hills and Valley is a Peace that unravels our knitted brow and quiets the nerves of our hand and restores in us the zest to live.

Then we will behold the misty crown of the Great Smokies. Surrounded by the beauties of Nature in her various robes of color, white, green-blue, and blue-gold, and patterns of red and brown constantly changing by the rays of the sun and the shadows, she gives you a new dedication of service and there will come to you a feeling of exaltation for you were there.

by John Locke

DIE GREAT SMOKY MOUNTAINS VIER JAHRESZEITEN VOLLER PRACHT

Der beliebteste Nationalpark Amerikas - 800 Quadratmeilen, etwa 60 Meilen lang und 20 Meilen breit, liegt zwischen der Westgrenze von North Carolina und der östlichen Grenze von Tennessee.

Dieser einzigartige Urlaubsort, weitab vom dichtbesiedelten Osten Amerikas, wird jährlich von beinahe 12 Millionen - Touristen besucht, also mehr als doppelt so viel wie die Besucherzahl jedes anderen amerikanischen Nationalparks.

DIE GRÜNDE DIESER BESONDEREN BELIEBTHEIT?

Geologieforscher wissen zu berichten, daß hier, im Gebiet der Appalachen, vor mehr als zweihundert Millionen Jahren durch eine große Erhebung des Erdbodens aus einem flachen See die Smoky Mountains entstanden sind.

Zweihundert Millionen Jahre lang tat dann die Erosion über Wind und Wasser ihr Werk, und die heute existierenden Täler und Hänge entstanden, so daß die Great Smoky Montains heute auf 16 über 6.000 Fuß hohe Berge und 53 über 5.000 hohe Gipfel zählen kann. Die Täler sind an ihrer tiefsten Stelle im Westen am Albrama Creek 857 Fuß tief, und das Gelände zieht sich dann in einer Abfolge von Tälern und Bergen bis hin zum 6.642 Fuß hohen Clingmans Dome, dem höchsten Punkt des Parkes.

Eine herrlich schöne Landschaft, in der sich tiefe Schluchten, sanfte Hänge, reissende Wildbäche, klare Seen, schroffe Felsen, dichte Wälder und grüne Weiden abwechseln.

Die üppige Flora des Parks bietet dem Besucher 1.300 verschiedene Arten von blühenden Sträuchern und Gewächsen, 130 verschiedene Baumarten sowie fast 30 Orchideenarten und Gräser jeder Spezies. Ein fruchtbarer Erdboden, ein großzügiger Regen (etwa 80 Fuß Niederschlag) und nicht zuletzt eine prächtige Sonne machen den Park zu einem der schönsten Naturparadiese Amerikas und der Welt.

Die üppige Vegetation (der Park ist dicht bewachsen mit Rhododendron und Berglorbeer) läßt zusammen mit dem Öl der Pinie einen charakteristischen Duft entstehen, der, mit einem leichten Nebel vermischt, bis zu den Bergspitzen aufsteigt, um dann wieder bis in die Tiefen der Täler hinabzusinken und auf diese Art den Great Smoky Montains wie dem Nationalpark ihren Namen zu geben.

So ist es kein Wunder, wenn unsere gefiederten Freunde zusammen mit Süßwasserfischen und den Tieren der Hügel und Täler, genau wie die Besucher des Parks, hier ein ungestörtes, einzigartiges Paradies vorfinden.

An dieser Stelle soll geschildert werden, wie die "Smokies" zum amerikanischen Naturschutzgebiet wurden. Wie Sie wissen werden, wurden alle anderen Naturschutzgebiete von der Regierung abgesondert, so daß Besitzansprüche durch Privatpersonen ausgeschlossen werden konnte.

Bei den Smokies war dies jedoch nicht der Fall. Für lange Zeit war das Gelände, das den besten Baumbestand Amerikas aufweist, Eigentum von Privatleuten und Forstgesellschaften. Bald versuchten zahlreiche Forstunternehmen, im Namen des Dollars die Bestände an Fichten, Tannen, Hemlocktannen, Eichen, Nußbaum und weiteren edlen Hölzern ausbeuteten. Mit ihren Sägewerken begannen diese Gesellschaften, eine der herrlichsten Nauturlandschaften Amerikas zu zerstören.

Doch Amerika war immer schon das Land tatkräftiger Männer, die überall da einschreiten, wo Hilfe gebraucht wird. Im Fall der Smoky Montains war es eine Frau, Mrs. Willis P. Davis aus Knoxville, Tennessee, die eine Bewegung gründete, um das einzigartige Gelände zum nationalen Naturschutzgebiet zu deklarieren.

Ihr folgten weitere Naturfreunde wie John D. Rockefeller jr. (Mitglied einer Famile, die auch heute noch überall da, wo es der Allgemeinheit zugute kommt, mit Investitionen in Millionenhöhe hilft) und stellten dem Projekt insgesamt 5.000.000.00 Dollar zur Verfügung. Diese Summe trug zusammen mit staatlichen, bundesstaatlichen und privaten Mitteln dazu bei, daß das Gebiet der Smokies angekauft und dem Bundesstaat übergeben werden konnte. So wurde am 8. September 1940 der Great Smoky Montains National Park geboren, der dem damaligen Präsidenten Franklin D. Roosevelt gewidmet war.

Der ungehemmten Entforstung der Smokies konnte Einhalt geboten werden, und es entstand ein herrliches Naturschutzgebiet, das allen Besuchern Beschaulichkeit, Ruhe und Erholung bietet.

Amerika, die Heimat von über zweihundertsiebzig Millionen Menschen, hatte der Welt eine beispielhafte Haltung demonstriert.

"Es gibt Augenblicke, an denen es unsere Pflicht ist, der Zerstörung unserer natürlichen Lebensquellen Einhalt zu gebieten, um der Natur, die uns großartige Berge und Schluchten, friedliche Täler, klare Seen und reißende Wildbäche bietet, eine Chance zu geben. Diese Natur gehört nicht uns, sondern unseren Nachfolgern, und muß darum in ihrer Einzigartigkeit unberührt gelassen werden."

Die friedliche Atmosphäre, die die Hügel und Täler der Great Smoky Mountains ausstrahlen, vertreibt uns alle Sorgen, beruhigt unsere vom Alltag angespannten Nerven und schenkt uns neue Lebenslust.

Betrachten wir also die neblige Krone der Great Smokies. Inmitten einer herrlichen Natur wechselt sie durch das Spiel der Schatten und Sonnenstrahlen ihr weißes, grünblaues, blaugoldenes und machmal auch rotbraunes Kleid und schenkt uns ein erhebendes Gefühl der Ausgeglichenheit und der Freude am Leben.

Von John Locke

LES GREAT SMOKY MOUNTAINS QUATRE SAISONS DE SPLENDEURS

Le Parc national le plus célèbre des Etats Unis - 800 miles carrés de superficie - environ 60 miles de long et 20 de largeur - à cheval sur la frontière Ouest de la Caroline du Nord et de la frontière Est du Tenessee.
Un merveilleux lieu de vacances pour la région Est très peuplée du pays. Environ 12 millions de visiteurs par an - plus de deux fois le nombre de ceux qui visitent n'importe quel autre parc en Amérique.

ET VOUS POURRIEZ VOUS DEMANDER: MAIS POURQUOI ?

Nos géologues nous disent qu'il y a plus de deux cents millions d'années la surface de la terre dans cette région des Appalaches connut un grand bouleversement et les Great Smokies se formèrent à partir d'une mer à bas-fonds.
Pendant ces millions d'années l'érosion de l'eau et du vent fit son oeuvre. C'est alors que se formèrent les vallées et les pentes qui existent aujourd'hui - on compte 16 cîmes de plus de 6.000 pieds et 53 qui dépassent 5.000 pieds de hauteur - . L'altitude des vallées part de 857 pieds à Abraham Creek, puis ces dernières montent et s'étalent en un déploiement de vallées et cîmes qui culminent à 6.642 pieds à Clingmans Dome, la montagne la plus élevée du parc.
Tout cela forme un panorama splendide. Vous y trouverez des gorges profondes, des pentes douces, des torrents rapides, des plans d'eau limpides, des roches déchiquetées, de grandes forêts et de riches prairies.
La flore y est luxuriante: on a recensé 1300 espèces d'arbustes à fleurs, 130 espèces d'arbres, environ 30 variétés d'orchidées et des plantes grasses de toutes sortes. Nourrie par un sol riche, par des pluies abondantes (environ 80 inches/an) et par le soleil de nos régions les plus tempérées, la végétation de ce parc en fait l'une des zones les plus luxuriantes du Monde, le Cachemire, le Shangri-La d'Amérique.
La croissance de cette végétation (qui inclut les rhododendrons et le laurier de montagne) s'associe aux huiles des pins pour exsuder un arôme et une vapeur qui s'élèvent et se mélangent aux moutonnements légers du brouillard. Celui-ci s'accroche aux cîmes des montagnes et s'enfonce dans la vallée, pour créer ainsi les *Smokies*, d'où le nom du Parc: le Parc National des *Great Smoky Mountains*.
Il n'est pas étonnant que nos amis ailés, tout comme les poissons qui aiment les eaux limpides et les animaux des collines et des profondes gorges apprécient ce parc et s'y joignent à nous, les humains, pour en faire leur hâvre et leur refuge.
Laissez-nous vous raconter comment les *Smokies* sont devenues l'un de nos Parcs nationaux. Comme vous le savez la plupart des autres Parcs furent organisés à partir de terres appartenant à l'Etat et avant que des particuliers n'aient eu le temps de réclamer un quelconque droit de propriété sur celles-ci. Toutefois, avec les *Smokies* ce fut différent. Pendant des années ces territoires ont appartenu à des particuliers et à des sociétés de bois de construction car on y trouvait l'une des plus vastes étendues de forêts des Etats Unis. Epicéas, sapins, chênes, noyers et autres arbres de grande qualité poussaient droits et hauts. Puis vint la force destructrice de l'homme à la recherche des bonnes affaires en monnaie sonnante et trébuchante. Des entreprises privées, en l'occurrence des scieries, commençaient à détruire l'une des plus belles régions sauvages du pays.
Par chance, l'une des raisons pour lesquelles nous sommes une grande nation et un grand peuple tient au fait qu'au moment du besoin il y a toujours eu quelqu'un qui est venu à notre secours. Dans le cas présent, ce fut une femme, Madame Willis P. Davis de Knoxville, Tennessee, qui, ayant réalisé l'importance de la zone, lança un mouvement pour sa transformation en Parc national.
D'autres suivirent, et John D. Rockefeller Jr. (membre d'une famille qui a donné et donne encore des sommes énormes aux zones qui en ont besoin, et où le bien-être public devrait être augmenté), a contribué pour 5.000.000,00 de USD à cette entreprise. Cet argent est allé s'ajouter aux fonds dégagés par l'Etat d'une part, et récolté par les Sources Privées et Fédérales par ailleurs: les terres des Smokies furent ainsi achetées et données au Gouvernement Fédéral. Le 8 septembre 1940 le Parc National des *Great Smoky Mountains* devint une réalité et fut officiellement inauguré par le Président Franklin D. Roosevelt.
Et voilà: les grands camps de bois de construction des Smokies furent bloqués et la richesse de cette zone fut transformée en un endroit de beauté et de tranquillité, un refuge contre tous ceux qui auraient pu arriver.
Et cette leçon fut enseignée à l'Amérique, notre maison, celle de plus de deux cents soixante dix millions d'individus comme nous. Il faut quelquefois crier très fort pour arrêter la destruction des ressources naturelles, nous devons donner une chance à la nature, car dans son plan elle a créé des cîmes et des gorges profondes et des vallées pacifiques, des lacs limpides ainsi que des torrents. Tout cela ne nous appartient pas, mais appartient à d'autres qui pourraient venir et il faut que ce grand projet reste inchangé".
La Paix que l'on trouve dans ces collines et dans ces vallées est celle qui efface nos rides, calme nos nerfs et redonne du sel à notre vie.
Alors voici les crêtes brumeuses des *Great Smokies* . Entourées des beautés de la Nature dans ses différents atours, blancs, vert-bleu et bleu-or et les lignes de rouge et de brun changeant constamment à cause des rayons de soleil et des ombres, elles vous donnent un nouveau sens du devoir et voici que naît en vous un sentiment d'exaltation comme si vous y étiez.

de John Locke

EL GREAT SMOKY MOUNTAINS CUATRO ESTACIONES DE ESPLENDOR

El más popular Parque Nacional de América - 800 millas cuadradas de superficie, cerca de 60 millas de longitud, 20 millas de ancho que cavalgan el confín oeste de Carolina del Norte y el confín este del Tennessee.
Una magnífica zona de vacaciones para el populoso este de nuestra Nación. Cerca de 12 millones de visitantes por año - más del doble de la cantidad de visitantes de cualquier otro parque nacional de América.

Y UD. SE PREGUNTARA, ¿PORQUÉ?

Nuestros geólogos nos han contado que hace más de doscientos millones de años, se produjo una gran alteración de la superficie de la Tierra en esta zona de los Apalaches y el Great Smokies se formó a partir de un mar poco profundo.
En esos millones de años la erosión del agua y del viento hicieron su trabajo. Se formaron los valles y pendientes actualmente existentes - y ahora nos encontramos con 16 picos que superan los 6.000 pies de altura y 53 sobre los 5.000 pies.
Los valles se alinean a partir de un bajo nivel de 857 pies en Abrams Creek en el Oeste y ascienden en una hilera quebrada de valles y picos hasta alcanzar los 6.642 pies en Clingman's Dome, la montaña más alta del parque.
Todo esto contribuye a crear un bellísimo panorama. Dentro de sus límites se encuentran gargantas profundas, suaves colinas, veloces cursos de agua, estanques transparentes, rocas recortadas, grandes bosques y ricos prados.
La vida vegetal es pródiga. Existen 1.300 clases de plantas y arbustos floridos, 130 diferentes clases de árboles, cerca de 30 variedades de orquídeas y hierbas de todo tipo. Nutrida por un rico suelo, por las frecuentes lluvias, (cerca de 80 pulgadas), y por el sol de nuestra región más templada, el area de este parque es una de las más lujuriosas del mundo, la Cachemira, el Shangri-La de América.
El abundante desarrollo vegetal (que acomuna el Rododendro y el Laurel de Montaña) combinado con el aceite de los pinos desprende aromas y vapores que suben y se mezclan con la liviana masa de niebla; la cual, ascendiendo hasta la cima de las montañas y descendiendo hacia el valle, constituye una masa fumosa de donde viene el nombre de Great Smoky Mountains National Park.
No es extraño que nuestros pequeños amigos, el pez que ama las aguas claras y los animales de las colinas y gargantas vengan al parque y se reunan con nosotros, la gente, convirtiendo al parque en su puerto y refugio. Les contaremos ahora como fue que Smokies se convirtió en uno de nuestros parques nacionales. Como es sabido, la mayoría de los otros parques fueron insediados en territorios del gobierno antes de que algún particular pudiera reclamar derechos sobre los mismos.
Sin embargo, en el caso de Smokies fue diferente. Durante años estas tierras fueron propiedad de particulares y de compañías madereras, dado que contiene una de las más preciadas extensiones de madera de Estados Unidos: abeto, cicuta, encina, nogal y otros árboles de maderas preciadas crecen rectos y fuertes. Entonces llegó la desvastadora fuerza del hombre en su búsqueda del dólar. Empresas privadas bajo la forma de aserraderos comenzaron a destruir una de las más maravillosas areas salvajes de la nación.
Afortunadamente, una de las razones por la cual somos una gran nación y un gran pueblo, es que en los momentos de necesidad siempre han aparecido individuos que nos han rescatado. En este caso una mujer, la Sra. Willa P. Davis de Knoxville, Tennessee, dándose cuenta de la grandeza del area puso en marcha un movimiento para transformar todo el complejo en un Parque Nacional.
Otros la siguieron, y John D. Rockefeller Jr. (un miembro de la familia que ha dado y aún dá millones para areas que lo necesitan, a favor del bienestar público), contribuyó con $5.000.000.000. Esta suma se agregó a los fondos provenientes del Estado, Federales y Privados y las tierras de Smokies fueron compradas y entregadas al Gobierno Federal. El 8 de Septiembre de 1940, el Great Smoky Mountains National Park se convirtió en una realidad cuando fue formalmente inaugurado por el Presidente Franklin D. Roosevelt.
Si, los grandes campos de madera de Smokies eran silenciosos y calmos y la riqueza del area fue canalizada para constituir un lugar de relax, de belleza y de refugio para todo aquél que se avecina.
Y América, nuestro hogar, el hogar de más de doscientos setenta millones de personas como nosotros, aprendió la lección.
"Hay momentos en los cuales debemos poner un freno a la destrucción de nuestros recursos naturales, debemos dar una posibilidad a la naturaleza, porque en su gran diseño ella ha construido picos y grandes gargantas, valles serenos, lagos transparentes y veloces cursos de agua. Esto no pertenece solo a nosotros sino también a otros que vendrán y nosotros debemos mantener intacto ese gran diseño."
La paz de estos valles y colinas es una paz que afloja nuestro ceño fruncido, calma los nervios de nuestras manos y restablece el gusto de vivir.
Estamos ante las brumosas cimas de Great Smokies. Circundados por la belleza de la naturaleza en sus diversos ropajes de color blanco, verde-azulado y azul dorado, con manchas de rojo y marrón siempre cambiantes en el juego de sol y sombras, se experimenta una nueva forma de relación con la misma y se produce en nosotros un sentimiento de exaltación por encontrarnos aquí.

John Locke

グレートスモーキー山岳国立公園
絢爛豪華な四季

アメリカの最も有名な国立公園（面積 800平方マイル− 長さ約60マイル− 幅約20マイル）は，ノースカロライナ州の西端，テネシー州の東端にまたがり広がっている．

住宅の密集したわが国東部における素晴らしい保養地の一つである．年間1千万人，日に7万人にも及ぶ人々が訪れるが，これは，他のアメリカ国内のどの国立公園よりも2倍以上にあたる訪問者数である．

なぜだと思われるだろうか．

地質学者たちによると2億年以上前，このアパラチアン地方に大きな造山運動が起こり，グレートスモーキー連山が海の浅瀬から形成されたとのことである．その後何百万年もの間，風雨による浸蝕がなされ今日存在する渓谷と斜面が形成される．現在6000フィート以上の高峰を16と，5000フィート以上の峰を53数える．渓谷は，西のアブラハムズ川流域で標高857フィートと最も低い地点を記録し，不規則な連山へと広がり，公園内での最高峰，6642フィートのクリングマンズドームがその頂点を成している．

これら全ての造形が美のパノラマである．この境界内に深い峡谷，なだらかなスロープ，急流，澄んだ泉，荒々しい岩，大きな森林，豊かな草原がある．

植物の群生はおびただしい．1300種の花の咲く低木があり，130種の樹木があり，30種ほどの柳とあらゆる種類の草が見られる．肥沃な土壌と多雨（80インチ）に培われ，温和な太陽がこの公園の地域を世界で最も恵み豊かな楽園，アメリカのカシミール，シャングリラと成している．植物の旺盛な繁茂（シャクナゲ科の植物の宝庫）に松の樹脂が加わり，芳香と蒸気を発散し，微かな淡い霧と交じり合って辺り一帯にたちのぼる．この芳香の霧が山の頂上をぴったりと覆い，谷間をゆっくりと下る．これがグレートスモーキー山岳国立公園の，スモーキーの名の由来である．我々の軽やかな仲間たち，澄んだ水を好む魚，丘や峡谷の動物たちがこの公園にやって来て人々と合流し，安息の地，憩いの地としているのは少しも不思議ではない．

ここ，スモーキーがどうやって我々の国立公園になったかをお話したい．ご存じのようにほとんどの他のアメリカの公園は，公有地から設定されているが，以前は個人がその内部に所有権を主張することも可能であった．

しかし，スモーキー公園の事情は違っている．長い間，この地区は複数の個人と合衆国随一の木材産地として木材会社に所有されていた．トウヒ，モミ，ベイツガ，オーク，ウォルナットなどの素晴らしい木々が高く直立して繁茂していた．そして，利潤追求のための人間による破壊の力が及び，製材企業が国内の自然の最も美しい地域の一つを破壊し始めた．

幸運なことに，我国と人々の偉大さの一つの理由でもあるが，必要時に常に誰かが保護に乗り出すのである．ここでは，一人の女性，テネシー州ノックスビルのウィリス・P・ディヴィス夫人がこの変化に富む総合的な地区を国立公園に変える運動を始めたことで，壮大な計画を実現する．他の人々がこれに続く．ジョン・D・ロックフェラー・Jr（現在でも多量の資金を必要とするこの地区，公共福祉が強化され得るであろうこの公園に何百万ドルの寄付をし続けている家族の一員）が500万ドルを寄付する．この資金に，国，州と個人の寄付金が加えられ，スモーキーの土地が購入され，合衆国政府に手渡された．1940年9月8日，グレートスモーキー山岳国立公園は現実となり，正式にフランクリン・D・ルーズベルト大統領によりオープニングの式典が執行なわれた．

現在でもスモーキーの偉大な木材産地は存在し，この地域の豊かさはリラックスの場として，自然美を愛でる場として，安息の場として，訪問者全てに開放されている．

この我祖国，我々のような2億7千万人以上の人間の祖国，アメリカは，この事実から多くを学んだ．"貴重な財産である自然破壊にストップを掛けるべき時があることを．山頂を，壮大な峡谷を，穏やかな谷間を，澄んだ湖，奔流を造った偉大なる自然の営みにチャンスを与えるべきであることを．これらは我々のみに属するのでなく，ここに来ることのできる全ての人間のものであり，破壊からぜひとも守らねばならないことを．"

この丘陵や渓谷のやすらぎは，我々のひそめた眉を広げさせ，我々の手の神経を緩め，我々に心地好い人生の刺激を蘇らせる．

白，エメラルドグリーン，金色がかったブルー，太陽の光線と影で常に変化する赤とブラウンの色調など自然の美しさ，様々な色の衣に取り巻かれてグレートスモーキーの霧の王冠を観察しよう．ここはあなたに新しいタイプのリラックスを提供し，あなたの中に，ここにいる喜びを沸き上がらせるに違いない．

ジョン ラック

TRANS MOUNTAIN HIGHWAY

From the highest point in the Smokies (6643'), a visitor can see a vision of delight from the top of Clingman's Dome. On clear days, Georgia, South Carolina, Virginia, and Tennessee are visible from this western North Carolina vantage point.

Vom höchsten Gipfel der Smokies aus (6643') hat man eine herrliche Sicht auf den Clingman's Dome. An klaren Tagen kann man von diesem günstigen Aussichtspunkt West Carolinas Georgia, Süd-Carolina, Virginia und Tennessee sehen.

Du point culminant des Smokies (6643'), un visiteur peut avoir une vue enchanteresse du haut de Clingman's Dome. Par temps clair, on peut distinguer du haut de ce magnifique coin de la Caroline du Nord, les paysage la Georgie, la Caroline du Sud, la Virginie et le Tenessee.

En el punto más alto de Smokies (6643'), un visitante puede tener una deliciosa vision desde la cima de Clingman's Dome. En los dias claros Georgia, Carolina del Sur, Virginia y Tennessee son visibles desde esta ventajosa ubicacion, al oeste de Carolina del Norte.

スモーキー山地の最も高い地点（6643マイル）から魅惑的なクリングマンズドームの眺望を楽しめる．晴れた日はノースカロライナ州のこの豪勢な展望台からはジョージア州サウスカロライナ州，バージニア州テネシー州を見渡すことができる．

Snow capped Mt. LeConte as seen from the Trans Mountain Highway near the Great Smoky Mountains Visitors Center.
Mt. LeConte (6593') emerges from out of the clouds in the horizon as seen from Clingman's Dome.

Die verschneite Spitze des LeConte, von der Panoramastraße nahe der Besucherstation der Great Smoky Mountains aus gesehen.
Blick vom Clingman's Dome auf den LeConte (6593'), der am Horizont aus den Wolken ragt.

La cime du Mont LeConte enneigée, vue de la route panoramique non loin du Centre Visiteurs des Great Smoky Mountains.
Le Mont LeConte (6593') perce les nuages à l'horizon, vu du Clingman's Dome.

La cima nevada del Monte LeConte vista desde la carretera panorámica el los alrededores del Centro Visitantes de las Great Smoky Mountains.
El Monte LeConte (6593') que emerge de entre las nubes al horizonte, visto desde el Clingman's Dome.

雪化粧したレコンテ山の頂き．グレートスモーキー山岳地帯内の
ビジターズセンターから行くパノラマ道よりの景観．
クリングマンズドームより望む，雲間から聳え立つ
レコンテ山（6593マイル）．

Mt. LeConte

The path to Alum Cave Bluff encircles the visitor with a forest of Fraser firs along the approach to LeConte Lodge.
The Appalachian Trail extends from Georgia to Maine, Charlie's Bunion marks a portion of the trail inside of the Great Smoky Mountains.

Besucher, die den Weg nach Alum Cave Bluff gehen, gelangen am Aufstieg zur LeConte-Hütte in einen dichten Fichtenwald.
Der Appalachen-Weg windet sich von Georgia bis nach Maine. Charlie's Bunion prägt seinen Abschnitt in den Great Smoky Mountains.

Le visiteur qui emprunte le sentier menant à la Alum Cave Bluff plonge dans une forêt de sapins tout le long de la voie qui mène au Refuge Leconte.
Le Sentier appalachien se déroule de la Georgie au Maine: Charlie's Bunion caractérise une partie du sentier à l'intérieur des Great Smoky Moutains.

El visitante que recorre el sendero que conduce a la Alum Cave Bluff está rodeado por un bosque de abetos durante todo el camino de acceso al Refugio LeConte.
El Sendero Apalache va desde Georgia hasta el Maine: Charlie's Bunion caracteriza una parte del sendero en el interior de las Great Smoky Mountains.

アラン　ケーブ　ブラッフへ導いてくれる小路を行くと，レコンテの山小屋への山道は，モミの木の森林の真っ直中を通る．アパラチア山脈はジョージア州からメーン州にまで渡って横たわる．チャーリーズ　バニォンは，グレートスモーキー山岳地帯内の一部の特徴を代表する場所である．

Clingman's Dome is the highest peak in the park, 6643', and the third highest in the Eastern United States. On a clear day Georgia, South Carolina, Virginia, and Tennessee are visible from this Western North Carolina vantage point.

Clingman's Dome ist mit 6643' die höchste Erhebung des Naturparks und die dritthöchste der gesamten östlichen USA. An klaren Tagen hat man von dieser günstigen Stelle in Nord-Carolina Sicht bis nach Georgia, Süd-Carolina, Virginia und Tennessee.

Avec ses 6643', Clingman's Dome est le plus haut sommet du parc et le troisième de la côte Est des Etats-Unis. Par beau temps, de ce site favorable de la Caroline du Nord, on aperçoit la Georgie, la Caroline du Sud, la Virginie et le Tennessee.

Clingman's Dome es la cima más alta de todo el parque y con sus 6643' es la tercera de los Estados Unidos Orientales. En los dias serenos, desde esta magnífica posición en Carolina del Norte, es posible ver la Georgia, Carolina del Sur, Virginia y Ténnesis.

クリングマンズドームは 6643 マイル と公園内で最も高く，合衆国東部では3番目の高さを誇る．晴れた日にはこのノースカロライナの展望台からはジョージア州，サウスカロライナ州，バージニア州，テネシー州が見渡せる．

Famous Loopover

The icy fingers of winter are warmed by the rising sun as the clouds provide a blanket to the mountains inside of the Great Smoky Mountains National Park.

Die sinkende Sonne erwärmt die eisigen Finger des Winters; dahinter liegen, in Wolken gehüllt, die Berge des Great Smoky Mountains - Nationalparks.

Les doigts gelés de l'hiver se réchauffent sous le soleil couchant, alors que les nuages enveloppent les montagnes de leur manteau, à l'intérieur du Parc National des Great Smoky Mountains.

Los dedos helados del Invierno se calientan con el sol del atardecer, mientras las nubes cubren las montañas con su manto, en el interior del Parque Nacional y de las Great Smoky Mountains.

グレートスモーキー山岳国立公園内で雲が再び山に衣を着せようとする頃、冬の凍りつく指を沈み行く太陽が暖める。

The Oconaluftee Visitors Center was created
from original buildings located throughout
the park. On display are pioneer artifacts
from over two centuries of life in the
Smokies.

Die Besucherstation Oconaluftee wurde aus
den Resten historischer Bauten des Parks
errichtet. Dort sind Handwerksarbeiten der
Siedler aus mehr als 200 Jahren Leben in den
Smokies ausgestellt.

El Centro Visitantes Oconaluftee ha sido
realizado utilizando los edificios originales
situados por todo el parque. Están expuestos
objetos hechos a mano por los pioneros,
recogidos durante más de dos siglos de vida
vivida en las Smokies.

Le Centre Visiteurs Oconaluftee a été
aménagé dans les bâtisses d'origine
disséminées dans le parc. On peut y admirer
des objets fabriqués par les pionniers des

オコナラフティビジターズセンターは，公園内全体に散在
するオリジナルの家をそのまま利用している．
スモーキー山中での2世紀以上に渡る開拓者の日常品，

A frosty blanket of snow and beautiful blue sky surround Mingus Mill. Freshly ground corn meal is available from this functioning water-driven turbine mill.

Ein Vorhang aus gefrorenem Schnee und ein herrlicher blauer Himmel umrahmen die Mingus - Mühle. Diese Wassermühle ist heute noch in Betrieb; man erhält dort frisch gemahlenes Weizenmehl.

Un rideau de neige glacée et un splendide ciel bleu encadrent le Moulin Mingus. Dans ce moulin à eau, qui fonctionne encore, on peut obtenir de la farine tout juste moulue.

Un manto de nieve helada y un esplendido cielo azul rodean el Molino Mingus. De este molino a turbina de agua, actualmente en función, se puede obtener harina de trigo apenas molida.

ミンガスの水車を取り囲む凍った雪のカーテンと眩しい青空. 現在でも使用されているこの水車で挽きたての小麦粉を手に得ることができる.

The buildings at the Oconaluftee
Visitors Center are heavy with snow as
a powdery mist continues to accumulate.

Die Gebäude der Besucherstation
Oconaluftee liegen schwer
schneebeladen; der Nebel verdichtet
sich zunehmend.

Les bâtiments du Centre Visiteurs
Oconaluftee sont lourds de neige,
alors que la brume devient de plus en
plus dense.

Los edificios del Centro Visitantes
Oconaluftee están cubiertos de nieve,
mientras la niebla es siempre más
espesa.

霧がますます濃さを増す中,
雪の降り積もったオコナラフティビジターズ
センター内の建物.

CATALOOCHEE VALLEY

Mother nature begins her masterpiece along peaceful country lanes with palettes of yellow, red and orange in the Cataloochee Valley.

Mutter Natur beginnt ihr Werk längs friedlicher Pfade und tupft das Cataloochee-Tal hier und dort mit Gelb, Rot und Orange.

L'oeuvre de Mère Nature commence le long de sentiers pacifiques, où elle rajoute ça et là quelques touches de jaune à la Vallée Cataloochee.

Madre naturaleza inicia su obra de arte a lo largo de los pacíficos senderos, retocando aquí y allá el Valle Cataloochee de amarillo, rojo y naranja.

大自然の母が穏やかな山道に沿って
カタルーチー渓谷のそこここに
パレットの黄，赤，オレンジを，流し込む．

The history of Cataloochee mirrors much of the Southern Appalachian region. The Cherokees hunted, fished and lived throughout the area long before white men ever set foot in Cataloochee. The name "Cataloochee" was taken from the Cherokee word "Gad-a-lu-tsi" meaning standing up in ranks, a reference to the "ranks" of trees along the tops of the surrounding mountains. As the white man came into the area this became known as "Cataloochee".

Die Geschichte des Cataloochee steht stellvertretend für fast die gesamte südliche Appalachen-Region. Die Cherokee-Indiander jagten, fischten und lebten hier, lange bevor der weiße Mann Fuß in das Tal setzte. Der Name "Cataloochee" leitet sich vom Wort "Gad-a-lu-tsi" der Cherokee-Sprache her. Es bedeutet: sich in eine Reihe stellen, und meint die Baumreihen auf den umliegenden Bergrücken. Nach Ankunft der Weißen wurde die Gegend "Cataloochee" genannt.

L'histoire de Cataloochee réflète pratiquement toute la région appalachienne sud. Les indiens Cherokee chassaient, pêchaient et vivaient dans cette région avant que l'homme blanc n'arrive dans cette vallée. Le nom "Cataloochee" dérive de "Gad-a-lu-tsi", un terme Cherokee qui signifie s'élever en rang, comme le faisaient les arbres sur les sommets des montagnes environnantes. Après l'arrivée de l'homme blanc, cette région devint célèbre sous le nom de "Cataloochee".

La historia de Cataloochee refleja casi toda la región apalache meridional. Los Indios Cherokee cazaban, pescaban y vivían en toda esta zona mucho antes de que el hombre blanco llegara a este valle. El nombre "Cataloochee" deriva de la palabra, en lenguaje Cherokee "Gad-a-lu-tsi" que significa erguirse en fila, refiriéndose a la "fila" de árboles sobre la cima de las montañas que lo rodean. Con la llegada del hombre blanco, la zona fue conocida con el nombre de "Cataloochee".

カタルーチーの歴史は，アパラチア山脈地方南部のほぼ全てを物語る．インディアンのチェロキー族は白人がこの渓谷に足を踏み入れるずっと以前から，このあたりに居住し，狩猟，魚釣りをしていた．"カタルーチー"の名は周辺の山頂に立並ぶ木の列について言った"立並ぶこと"を意味するチェロキー語の"Gad-a-lu-tsi"から来ている．白人の到来以来，この地区は"カタルーチー"の名で知られている．

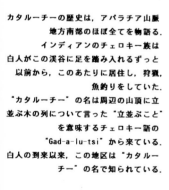

FONTANA

A fog laden mist encompasses the early dawn at Fontana Lake. In the early 1940's, Fontana Lake was created to satisfy the area's need for electricity.

Am frühen Morgen umsäumen dichte Nebelschwaden den Fontana-See. Anfang der 40-er Jahre hatte man diesen See zur Energieerzeugung geschaffen.

Une brume chargée de brouillard enveloppe le Lac Fontana aux premières lueurs de l'aube. Ce lac fut créé au début des années 40 pour répondre aux besoins énergétiques de la région.

Una calígine llena de niebla rodea el Lago Fuente en las primeras horas del alba. Este lago fue creado a principios de los años 40 en respuesta a la demanda energética de la zona.

黎明の湖を濃い霧が取り巻く. この人口湖は1940年代初頭に地区への エネルギー供給のために建設された.

Indian Creek Falls

LITTLE RIVER ROAD

Lush vegetation, rocks covered in moss, and cool waters of the Little Pigeon River delight the visitor along Little River Road.

Eine üppige Vegetation, moosüberzogene Felsen und die eisigen Wasser des Little Pigeon River erfreuen Besucher, die die Straße des Kleinen Flusses nehmen.

Une végétation luxuriante, des roches revêtues de mousse et les eaux gelées du Little Pigeon River égaieront la promenade des visiteurs qui empruntent la route du Petit Fleuve.

Una abundante vegetación, rocas cubiertas de musgo y las heladas aguas del Little Pigeon River alientan al visitante que recorre la carretera del Pequeño Rio.

鬱蒼と茂る木々，苔に覆われた岩の間を流れるリトル　ピジョン　リバーの冷たい水が，小渓流の路を行く訪問者を喜ばせる.

Laurel Falls received its name from Mountain Laurel, a wild flowering bush, found throughout the Smokies.
A colorful blend of oranges and yellows is a typical scene throughout the Smokies as witnessed from the Laurel Falls footpath.

Die Laurel-Wasserfälle heißen nach dem gleichnamigen Berg; eine wilde, blühende Landschaft in den Smokies.
Die Mischung aus Orange- und Gelbtönen ist typisch für die Smokies, wie man längs des Pfades am Laurel-Wasserfall sieht.

Les cascades Laurel doivent leur nom au mont omonyme, un site sauvage des Smokies.
Le mélange de tons orange et jaune est courant dans les Smokies, comme on peut s'en rendre compte en parcourant le sentier des Cascades Laurel.

Las cascadas Laurel han recibido el nombre del monte homónimo - terreno salvaje y floreciente que se encuentra en las Smokies.
La combinación de naranjas y amarillos es una escena típica de las Smokies, como se puede observar recorriendo el sendero de las Cascadas Laurel.

ローラルの滝はスモーキー山岳地帯にある野生味溢れる同名の山名を冠している.
ローラルの滝の路を行くと気がつくように，オレンジと黄のコンビネーションの風景はスモーキー山地の特色でもある.

Meigs Falls

Meigs Falls

FLORA OF THE

Butterfly Weed

Jack'n the Pulpit Seeds

Ragwort

Sundrops

Orange Fringed Orchid

Butterfly Peas

Fire Pink

GREAT SMOKY MOUNTAINS

Closed Gentian

Phlox

Pitcher Plant

Blue Spiderwort

Carolina Rose

CADES COVE

Often described as "a little bit a heaven", Cades Cove is one of the favorite destinations in the Great Smokies. This eleven mile one way loop road allows the visitor to step back in time to the nineteenth century. Along the route are one hundred fifty year old cabins, waterfalls, a grist mill, breathtaking scenery, deer, bear, and other animals.

Oft der "kleine Garten Eden" genannt, ist Cades Coves eins der beliebtesten Ziele in den Great Smokies. Die 11 Meilen lange, gewundene Straße führt den Besucher zurück in das 19. Jahrhundert. Er sieht 150 Jahre alte Häuser, Wasserfälle, eine Mühle, atemberaubende Ausblicke, Damwild, Bären und andere Tiere.

Souvent décrite comme un "petit paradis", Cades Cove est une des destinations favorites des Great Smokies. Cette route tortueuse de onze miles de long ramène le visiteur au XIXe siècle. On y rencontre des maisons construites il y a cent cinquante ans, des cascades, un moulin et, dans un paysage à couper le souffle, des daims, des ours et autres animaux.

A menudo descrita como un "pequeño Edén", Cades Cove es una de las metas favoritas de las Great Smokies. Esta carretera tortuosa, larga once millas, translada al visitante al siglo XIX. Se pueden encontrar, recorriéndola, residencias de hace cientocincuenta años, cascadas, un molino, gamos, osos y demás animales.

しばしば "小エデン" と呼ばれるケイズコーブはグレートスモーキーの最も有名な名所である．この曲がりくねった11マイルの路は訪問者を19世紀に誘う．150年前の家，滝，水車，息をのませるシーン，鹿，熊，その他の動物たちに行き交う．

The dazzling touch of Mother Nature's paintbrush fills the valley with color at Cades Cove.

Der wundervolle Pinselstrich von Mutter Natur erfüllt das Cades Cove -Tal mit Farben.

Le coup de pinceau exceptionnel de Mère Nature a coloré la vallée de Cades Cove.

El increible toque de pincel de Madre Naturaleza llena de colores el valle de Cades Cove.

驚嘆に値する，自然の，筆先のタッチが，ケイズ コーブの渓谷を様々な色影で染め 上げる．

As a new day begins, the smoky mist of lavender and pink envelope the Cades Cove Valley. Reflections of sunrise at Cades Cove glow in the small stream of the valley.

Ein neuer Tag bricht an. Das Cades Cove - Tal liegt in einen violetten und rosa Nebel gehüllt. In Cades Cove spiegelt sich das Morgenlicht im kleinen Talbach.

La naissance d'un nouveau jour. Une brume violette et rosée enveloppe la Vallée de Cades Cove. A Cades Cove, les reflets de l'aube se reflètent dans le petit ruisseau de la Vallée.

El despuntar del nuevo día. Una bruma morada y rosada cubre el Valle de Cades Cove. En Cades Cove, los reflejos del alba resplandecen en el pequeño torrente del valle.

新しき日の始まり，ラベンダーと桃色のもやが
ケイズ　コーブの谷間を包みこむ.
ケイズ　コーブで谷の渓流に朝の光が反射する.

The Dan Lawson Place stands to remind us of the hardy settlers who once inhabited these sturdy cabins through many a harsh winter.

Dan Lawson Place erinnert an die Siedler, die einst diese robusten Häuser viele strenge Winter lang bewohnten.

Dan Lawson Place a conservé le souvenir des colonisateurs qui, autrefois, habitèrent ces solides maisons pendant les longs hivers rigides.

Dan Lawson Place mantiene vivo el recuerdo de los colonos que en un tiempo vivieron en estas sólidas casas durante muchos rígidos inviernos.

ダン ローソン ブレースは，このような頑強な家で毎年，厳しい冬を過ごした開拓者の記憶を守る．

A pastoral scene as seen from Rich Mountain Road looking down into the Cades Cove.

Eine Hirtenszene, von der Rich Mountain Road im Cades Cove aus gesehen.

Scène pastorale vue de la Rich Mountain Road qui s'ouvre sur Cades Cove.

Una escena pastoril vista desde la Rich Mountain Road que se extiende sobre Cades Cove.

ケイズ　コーブを通過するリッチ マウンテン　ロードから見える牧歌的な 風景.

Covered with a coat of ice, the stark tree sparkles and glistens in the sunlight.

Dieser kahle Baum strahlt, von einer Eisschicht überzogen, im Sonnenlicht.

Recouvert d'une fine couche de glace, cet arbre dépouillé resplendit à la lumière du soleil.

Cubierto por una capa de hielo, este árbol desnudo resplandece a la luz del sol.

氷の薄層に包まれた裸の木が太陽の光に輝く.

FAUNA OF THE

Lunchtime

Red Fox

A Lovely Fawn

Cougar

Red Raccoon

GREAT SMOKY MOUNTAINS

Magnificent Deer

American Eagles

Baby Screech Owls

Black Bear

Curious Cub

ROARING FORK
NATURE TRAIL

South from Airport Road in Gatlinburg the Motor Nature Trail follows the Roaring Fork circling past the trails to Rainbow and Grotto Falls.

Südlich der Airport Road, in Gatlinburg, folgt der mit dem Auto befahrbare Naturpfad dem Roaring Fork und kreuzt den Weg zum Rainbow - und Grotto-Wasserfall.

Au sud d'Airport Road, à Gatlinburg, le Sentier Naturel ouvert à la circulation longe le Roaring Fork, au-delà des pistes qui mènent aux cascades Rainbow et Grotto.

Al sur de la Airport Road en Gatlinburg, el sendero natural que se puede recorrer en coche sigue el Roaring Fork superando las pistas que llevan a las cascadas Rainbow y Grotto.

ガットリンバーグのエアポート道路の南，ローリング フォークの先，虹と洞窟の滝へ行く路を越えると自然自動車道がある。

Junglebrook Homestead is located on the Cherokee Orchard-Roaring Fork Motor Trail. This well preserved homestead, Noah Ogle Farm, reminds us of a simpler lifetime.

Junglebrook Homestead liegt an der Cherokee Orchard-Roaring Fork Motor Trail. Dieses gut erhaltene Haus, die Noah Ogle Farm, weckt die Erinnerung an eine einfache Lebensart.

Junglebrook Homestead se trouve le long de la Cherokee Orchard-Roaring Fork Motor Trail. Noah Ogle Farm, une maison bien conservée, évoque le souvenir d'un style de vie simple.

Junglebrook Homestead se encuentra a lo largo de la Cherokee Orchard-Roaring Fork Motor Trail. Esta casa perfectamente conservada, la Noah Ogle Farm, recuerda un estilo de vida más sencillo.

ジャングルブルック　ホームステッドは Cherokee Orchard-Roaring Fork Motor Trail に沿ってある．この保存の状態の良好な家はノアオグル農場で，簡素なスタイルの生活の記憶を証言する．

ainbow Falls

Cosby Creek

Abrams Falls

Grotto Fal

From the trickle of Cosby Creek to the turbulent waters of Abrams Falls, the abundant waterfall has created lavish flora and fauna found throughout the Smokies.

Vom Tröpfeln des Cosby Creek zu den tosenden Wassern der Abramsfälle. Die vielen Wasserfälle haben in den Smokies eine reichhaltige Flora und Fauna hervorgebracht.

Du goutte à goutte de Cosby Creek aux eaux tumultueuses des Cascades Abrams, les nombreuses cascades des Smokies ont donné naissance à une flore et une faune splendides.

Desde el gotear de Cosby Creek hasta las turbulentas aguas de las cascadas Abrams. La abundancia de cascadas ha dado origen en todas las Smokies a una rica flora y fauna.

カズビー　クリークの飛沫から，アブラハムの滝の奔流．多くの滝がスモーキー山岳地帯全体を動植物の宝庫にしている．

62

Another day begins with a golden sunrise peaking over the mountain ridge.

Mit goldenem Sonnenaufgang bricht über der Bergkette ein neuer Tag an.

La naissance du jour avec l'aube dorée sur la chaîne montagneuse.

El despuntar de un nuevo día con un amanecer dorado sobre la cadena montañosa.

夜明けに，暁の金色の光が山脈を照らす.